Prayer Journal

HEY, GOD, LET'S TALK!

HEY, GOD, LET'S TALK!

ISBN 0-687-08351-6 (softcover)
0-687-03379-9 (hardcover)

Prayers on pages 6, 9, 18, 19, 21, 22, 23, 26, 27, 29, 30, 31, 33, 41, 42, 43, 48, 57, and 63 are from EVERYDAY PRAYERS FOR TEENS by Barry L Culbertson. Copyright © 1994 by Dimensions for Living. Used by permission.

Prayers on pages 8, 10, 11, 13, 17, 28, 38, and 39 are from A MOMENT WITH GOD FOR CHILDREN by Barbara Younger. Copyright © 1997 by Dimensions for Living. Used by permission.

Prayers on pages 47, 58, 59, 60, 61, and 62 are from A MOMENT WITH GOD FOR TEENS by Lisa Flinn. Copyright © 1997 by Dimensions for Living. Used by permission.

All Scripture quotations are from the New Revised Standard Version Bible, copyright © 1989, by the Division of Christian Education of the National Council of the Churches of Christ in the United States of America. Used by permission.

00 01 02 03 04 05 06 07 08 09—10 9 8 7 6 5 4 3 2 1

MANUFACTURED IN THE UNITED STATES OF AMERICA

PRESENTED

To_ _____

By___ _ _

Date_ ___

3

"Lord, teach us to pray."

Luke 11:1

PRAYER POINT

Prayer is a special way we talk to God and listen to God. There are different kinds of prayers.

What prayer means to me

_____

_____

_____

_____

_____

_____

_____

PRAYER PROMISE

God said, "I know you by name."

Exodus 33:17. adapted

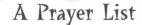

A Prayer List

God, here's my list. Each one
on the list is important to me today. I
believe you will understand what I
mean when I just say the word. OK?
I'm praying for:
the neighbor whose wife died
the hungry everywhere
the problem at school
Uncle Bill
my grades
Friday night
the words I said to Jill
the money I need
the test next week
That's about it.
Thanks for listening. Do
what you can through
my prayers. Help me keep
my eyes open to the help
you give. Thanks. Amen and
Amen.

ADORATION AND PRAISE:

Adoration means admiring what God has done for us; praising God for who God is and what God is doing and has done. It is praising God's greatness and accepting God's love. Giving God praise is one way of loving God.

Read Psalm 95:1-7 for an example of a prayer of praise.

CONFESSION:

Confession is telling God about something that we have done wrong or have not done and saying, "I'm sorry" for it. Confession is also asking God to help us avoid doing the same things again.

Read 1 John 1:9 for a promise about prayers of confession.

THANKSGIVING:

In this prayer, we express our gratitude for what God has done, God's love for us, and God's gifts to us.

Read Psalm 100 in your Bible for an example of this kind of prayer.

SUPPLICATION:

This is a big word for asking God's help for ourselves and for meeting our needs. We must remember that God hears our prayers, but may not answer them the way we expect. God knows us and knows our needs, even before we ask.

Read Psalm 70: 1-3, 5 for examples of this kind of prayer.

+PLUS

INTERCESSORY:

This is praying for others' desires and needs. When we pray for others, we are expressing love and care for them.

Read 2 Chronicles 30:18-19 for an example of this type of prayer.

A for **ADORATION AND PRAISE**

I offer my praise to God.

_____

_____

_____

_____

_____

_____

_____

Dear God, I like to make up brand new songs and sing them just for you. What a fun way to pray! Amen.

O come, let us sing to the LORD;
let us make a joyful noise to
the rock of our salvation!

Psalm 95:1

C for **CONFESSION**

I tell God that I am sorry and ask God's forgiveness.

_____

_____

_____

_____

_____

_____

Dear Lord, . . . forgive me when I do what you don't want me to do and don't do what you would have me do. . . . Amen.

> If we confess our sins, he who
> is faithful and just will forgive us
> our sins and cleanse us from all
> unrighteousness.
>
> _1 John 1:9_

T for **THANKSGIVING**

I offer my thanks to God for all God has done,
for God's love, and for God's gifts.

_____

_____

_____

_____

_____

_____

Dear God, With my paints, I just created a spectacular
rainbow—Red, Orange, Yellow, Green, Blue, and Purple. I'll hang
it on my door for everyone to admire, as a rainbow reminder
that you have painted our world with color. Amen.

O give thanks to the LORD, for he is good;

for his steadfast love endures forever.

Psalm 106:1

S for **SUPPLICATION**

I ask for God's help.

_____

_____

_____

_____

_____

_____

God, . . . when I am scared, help me to remember that I can
always trust in you. Thank you for helping me with my fears.

Turn to me and be gracious to me,
for I am lonely and afflicted.
Relieve the troubles of my heart,
and bring me out of my distress.

Psalm 25:16-17

+ I for **INTERCESSORY**

I pray for others' desires and needs.

_____

_____

_____

_____

_____

_____

Dear God, please watch over people who are sick or uneasy tonight. Bless them and bring them comfort. Be near to my family and friends. Amen.

The LORD watches over all who love him.

Psalm 145:20a

Dear God,

Bubbles burst,
balloons pop,
ice melts, and even
flowers don't last forever.
But the Bible
tells me
that you are
forever,
and that you
always
will be my
God.
Amen.

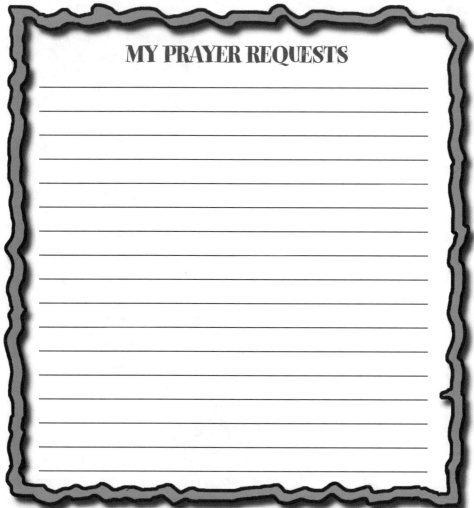

MY PRAYER REQUESTS

PRAYER POINT

I can pray in many different ways. The position and posture of my body communicates certain attitudes and feelings about prayer.

Dear God, I am thankful that I can talk to you in any place, time, or way.

_____

_____

_____

_____

_____

_____

_____

PRAYER PROMISE

The LORD is near to all who call upon him.

Psalm 145:18a

Ways to Pray

When I kneel to pray, I put myself in a humble position before God.

When I offer prayers of praise and thanksgiving, I may raise my arms with my hands open and upward to God.

When I open myself to receiving God's blessing, I stretch my arms outward in front of myself with my palms facing upward.

In times of deep distress, I may lie face down with my arms outstretched to form the shape of a cross while I ask for God's help.

Often I pray by going to my favorite place and sitting in quietness while I think about God.

Eyes open, eyes closed, sitting, standing, kneeling,
lying down, walking, running, skipping, alone—
or in a crowd—
God hears me when I pray at any time and in any place.

Dear God,
I can pray
to you
Anytime,
Anywhere,
About
anything
at all.
Now that's cool.
Amen.

A for **ADORATION AND PRAISE**

_____

_____

_____

_____

_____

_____

_____

God, as I lie here in my bed I praise you for this great day. . . .
In spite of the bad days (and some are awful! Remember?) I
still praise you for the good. Thanks for making good times
possible. Praise you and thanks again! Amen!

> Jumping up, he stood and began to walk,
> and he entered the temple with them,
> walking and leaping and praising God.
>
> _Acts 3:8b_

C for **CONFESSION**

_____

_____

_____

_____

_____

_____

_____

God, I told a joke today. It got a lot of laughs. I impressed my friends. But, I put somebody down in the joke. . . . Help me in my humor, O you who must know what it is to laugh! Amen.

Happy are those whose

transgression is forgiven.

Psalm 32:1

T for **THANKSGIVING**

_____

_____

_____

_____

_____

_____

_____

I am thankful, Lord, for my home and for those who love me.
Thank you for watching over me each day. Thank you for your
love that never ends. Amen.

Blessed be the LORD,

for he has wondrously shown

his steadfast love to me.

Psalm 31:21a

S for **SUPPLICATION**

_____

_____

_____

_____

_____

_____

_____

O God, . . . hear my sadness please. Today I struck out with a
runner on third. We went on to lose the game and no one felt
worse than I did. . . . Lord, I struck out! Hear my prayer.

> . . . they will return to the LORD,
> and he will listen to their
> supplications and heal them.
>
> _Isaiah 19:22b_

+ I for **INTERCESSORY**

_____

_____

_____

_____

_____

_____

_____

If only today God,
No guns would blaze, No hearts would ache,
No tears would fall, No graves would be dug. . . .
If only today God, I could help these come true.
Then heaven, God, then heaven. Amen.

Every generous act of giving,
with every perfect gift, is from above.

James 1:17

On the mountain,
in the valley, by the sea,
on the shore;
on the dance floor,
near the football field,
on the court;
in the church, in the classroom,
. . .
and while asleep;
watching TV, "kicking back,"
holding hands,
and slapping backs;
in quiet and with
stereo booming,
in sickness,
and in health,
whether sad or glad,
your name be praised!
Amen!

MY PRAYER REQUESTS

_____

_____

_____

_____

_____

_____

_____

_____

_____

_____

_____

_____

Do not worry about anything,
but in everything by prayer
and supplication with
thanksgiving let your requests
be made known to God.

Philippians 4:6

PRAYER POINT

Jesus prayed often and taught his followers about prayer. Through his teachings on prayer, I can learn how to pray.

Dear God, I ask your help in learning how to pray. Teach me how to put my whole self into my prayers. Help my words have meaning, so that my thoughts reach you. Be near to me every hour of every day. This is always my prayer.

_____

_____

_____

_____

_____

PRAYER PROMISE

"Ask, and it will be given you; search, and you will find; knock, and the door will be opened for you."

Matthew 7:7

THE A-S-K ACROSTIC

A for **ASK**
S for **SEARCH**
K for **KNOCK**

This acrostic reminds me not to be discouraged when I pray. I will keep on asking, searching, and knocking; for when I sincerely pray, I know that God hears my prayers.

I prayed today and no answer came.

I wonder.

I wait. I believe. I trust.

"I believe; help my unbelief!"
Mark 9:24

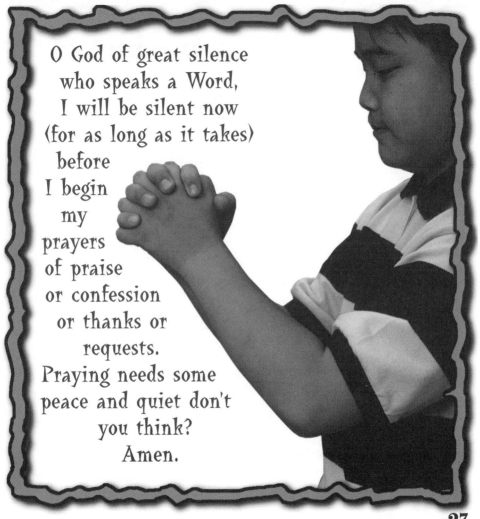

O God of great silence
who speaks a Word,
I will be silent now
(for as long as it takes)
before
I begin
my
prayers
of praise
or confession
or thanks or
requests.
Praying needs some
peace and quiet don't
you think?
Amen.

27

A for ADORATION AND PRAISE

_____

_____

_____

_____

_____

_____

_____

Dear God, I'm not at all surprised that you were pleased
when you finished creating the world. I'd be pleased, too, if I
could make a world like ours! Amen.

Let the heavens be glad, and let the earth rejoice;

let the sea roar, and all that fills it;

let the field exult, and everything in it.

Psalm 96:11-12a

C for **CONFESSION**

_____

_____

_____

_____

_____

_____

Oh, God, I've done it again. Gone and made Mom mad at me. She says she's not mad, but she's not talking to me very much. I said something I should have left unsaid. Forgive me. Help her to forgive me. . . . God, you are the one who can give me the better words for someone I really love and really didn't want to hurt. Help. Amen.

> In him we have redemption through his blood, the
> forgiveness of our trespasses, according to the riches
> of his grace that he lavished on us.
>
> _Ephesians 1:7-8_

T for **THANKSGIVING**

_____

_____

_____

_____

_____

_____

God, just a prayer for the snow. Beautiful! Nice work! And a day off from classes! Nice combination! Protect those who have to drive in all this. May they also see how beautiful it is even as they have to come and go in it. Thanks for the fun I intend to have real soon! God bless everyone in the snow! Amen!

Praise the LORD!
How good it is to sing praises to our God;
for he is gracious, and a song of praise is fitting.

Psalm 147:1

S for **SUPPLICATION**

_____

_____

_____

_____

_____

_____

_____

Understanding God, I have been hurt by someone who should have known better. . . . I feel betrayed and left out. . . . May I have the faith that Jesus goes with me when others have left me. Amen.

Pray in the Spirit at all
times in every prayer
and supplication.

Ephesians 6:18

+ I for **INTERCESSORY**

_____

_____

_____

_____

_____

_____

_____

God bless little children today everywhere on earth. Bless the children who are hungry, who have no home, and who need someone to love them. Bless the children who have too little and those who have too much. Amen.

"Blessed are the peacemakers,
for they will be called children of God."

Matthew 5:9

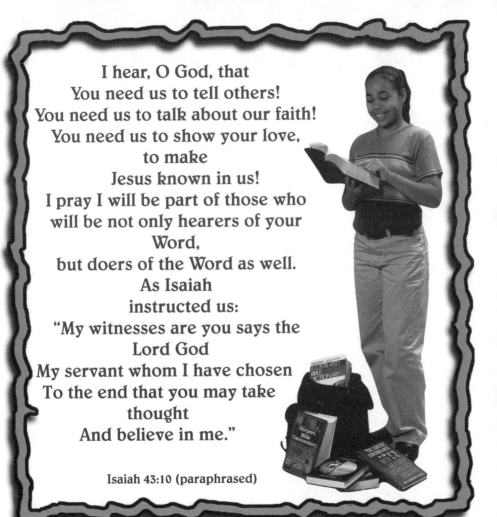

I hear, O God, that
You need us to tell others!
You need us to talk about our faith!
You need us to show your love,
to make
Jesus known in us!
I pray I will be part of those who
will be not only hearers of your
Word,
but doers of the Word as well.
As Isaiah
instructed us:
"My witnesses are you says the
Lord God
My servant whom I have chosen
To the end that you may take
thought
And believe in me."

Isaiah 43:10 (paraphrased)

MY PRAYER REQUESTS

_____

_____

_____

_____

_____

_____

_____

_____

_____

_____

_____

_____

_____

_____

Therefore confess your sins to one another, and pray
for one another, so that you may be healed. The
prayer of the righteous is powerful and effective.

James 5:16

The prayer Jesus taught his followers teaches me about my relationship with God and with other people.

Thank you for patterns that help me grow in my prayer life.

Our Father . . . *God loves me like a loving parent.*

Hallowed be Thy name . . . *I offer praise to God.*

Thy will be done . . . *Jesus taught us how to live.*

Give us this day . . . *God supplies my needs and I share with others.*

. . . forgive us . . . as we forgive . . . *When I have done wrong, God will forgive me. I follow God's example and forgive others.*

Lead us not into temptation, but deliver us from evil. *God will help me in the hard times of life.*

PRAYER PROMISE

Be still, and know that I am God.

Psalm 46:10

Our Father, who art in heaven,
hallowed be thy name.
Thy kingdom come,
thy will be done on earth
as it is in heaven.
Give us this day our daily bread,
And forgive us our trespasses,
as we forgive those who
trespass against us.
And lead us not into temptation,
but deliver us from evil.

Many churches around the world use these words when praying the Lord's Prayer. This basic form can be found in Matthew 6:9-13.

Our Father, who art in heaven,
hallowed be thy name.
Thy kingdom come,
thy will be done on earth
as it is in heaven.
Give us this day our daily bread.
And forgive us our trespasses
as we forgive
those who
trespass against us.
And lead us not
into temptation,
but deliver us
from evil.
For thine is the
kingdom, and the power,
and the glory,
forever. Amen.

Long ago the custom or tradition for using prayers in worship services was to end the prayer with praise to God. The last phrase, "For thine is the kingdom, and the power, and the glory, forever," was added to Matthew's accounting in order to end with praise to God.

A for **ADORATION AND PRAISE**

_____

_____

_____

_____

_____

_____

Dear God,

Morning, noon, and night, I praise you with all my might.
Thank you, Thank you, Thank you, Lord! Amen.

> I will bless the LORD at all times;
> his praise shall continually be
> in my mouth.
>
> *Psalm 34:1*

C for CONFESSION

_____

_____

_____

_____

_____

_____

Dear God,

I know that sometimes I do things that you
don't want me to do.
But I am a child who is willing to say, "I'm sorry."
And you are a God who forgives.
Amen.

> Now by this we may
> be sure that we know him, if
> we obey his commandments.
>
> _1 John 2:3_

T for **THANKSGIVING**

_____

_____

_____

_____

_____

_____

Thank you, Almighty Giver, for the earth that grows our food.
Thank you for the workers who plant and tend and harvest
and distribute it. Thank you for the life in every seed and every
cell. Amen.

> "As long as the earth endures,
> seedtime and harvest, cold and heat,
> summer and winter, day and night,
> shall not cease."
>
> _Genesis 8:22_

S for **SUPPLICATION**

_____

_____

_____

_____

_____

_____

_____

O God, words do hurt. _____ criticized me in front of everyone. I can't believe it. . . . If this is part of growing up and learning to get along, I'm not sure I can handle it. [Please help me, loving God.] Amen.

Help me, O LORD my God!

Save me according to your steadfast love.

Psalm 109:26

41

+ I for **INTERCESSORY**

_____

_____

_____

_____

_____

_____

_____

God of every nation and all people, I am saddened by the reports of so many hungry people throughout the world. . . . "Give us this day, our daily bread. . . ." It has been given, and I must find a way to share the bounty of the earth and the labor of our hands. Amen.

> Do not neglect to do good and to share what you have,
> for such sacrifices are pleasing to God.
>
> _Hebrews 13:16_

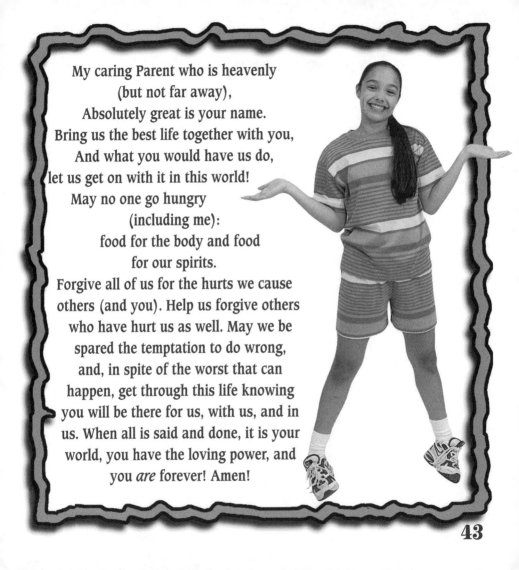

My caring Parent who is heavenly
(but not far away),
Absolutely great is your name.
Bring us the best life together with you,
And what you would have us do,
let us get on with it in this world!
May no one go hungry
(including me):
food for the body and food
for our spirits.
Forgive all of us for the hurts we cause
others (and you). Help us forgive others
who have hurt us as well. May we be
spared the temptation to do wrong,
and, in spite of the worst that can
happen, get through this life knowing
you will be there for us, with us, and in
us. When all is said and done, it is your
world, you have the loving power, and
you *are* forever! Amen!

MY PRAYER REQUESTS

_____

_____

_____

_____

_____

_____

_____

_____

_____

_____

_____

_____

_____

God is love, and those who abide in love abide in
God, and God abides in them.

1 John 4:16b

PRAYER POINT

Prayer was important to many people in the Bible. Bible people praised God and prayed prayers of confession and of thanksgiving. They asked for God's help for themselves and for others. God heard the prayers of Bible people and God hears my prayers.

Gracious God, how exciting it is to think that people my age long ago prayed to you and that you answered their prayers!

_____

_____

_____

_____

_____

_____

PRAYER PROMISE

Samuel said, "Speak, for your servant is listening."

1 Samuel 3:10b

The Prayer of St. Francis

Lord, make me an instrument of thy peace;
where there is hatred, let me sow love;
where there is injury, pardon;
where there is doubt, faith;
where there is despair, hope;
where there is darkness, light;
and where there is sadness, joy.

O Divine Master,
grant that I may not so much seek
to be consoled as to console;
to be understood, as to understand;
to be loved, as to love;
for it is in giving that
we receive,
it is in pardoning that we
are pardoned,
and it is in dying that we are
born to eternal life.

God,

The Bible says to be thankful at all times. This is hard to do, especially when I think that a situation is unfair. When I get angry, all kinds of negative thoughts come rushing into my mind.

But maybe that's the point of being thankful. If I could debate with myself, I'd ask, "What is good about what happened?"

I'll try to think positively, and maybe I'll find a solution, an alternative, or a new perspective. Amen.

Give thanks in all circumstances;
for this is the will of God in Christ Jesus for you.
1 Thessalonians 5:18

A for **ADORATION AND PRAISE**

_____

_____

_____

_____

_____

_____

_____

O Lord, what a great, magnificent, wonderful day! I'm alive and thankful! What more can I say? I can't because I just *feel* it! Thanks again! Amen.

From the rising of the sun to its setting
the name of the LORD is to be praised.

Psalm 113:3

C for CONFESSION

_____

_____

_____

_____

_____

_____

_____

_____

Dear God, sometimes I forget that others need to see you in me. Forgive me and help me to remember. Amen.

Humble yourselves before the Lord,
and he will exalt you.

James 4:10

T for **THANKSGIVING**

_____

_____

_____

_____

_____

_____

_____

_____

O God, I want to say thank you for the opportunity of learning. Help me to keep my eyes, ears, and heart open to see, to hear, and to receive. Amen.

> My child, do not forget my teaching,
> but let your heart keep my commandments.
>
> _Proverbs 3:1_

50

S for **SUPPLICATION**

_____

_____

_____

_____

_____

_____

Dear God, it's Monday again. I'm still sleepy from staying up late, I don't have all my homework done, and it looks like I will not get it finished. Help me through this day Lord, and help me to do better in the future. Amen.

To this day I have had help from God, and so I stand here, testifying to both small and great . . .

Acts 26:22

+ I for **INTERCESSORY**

_____

_____

_____

_____

_____

_____

_____

Dear loving God, bless everyone in this house. Bless all my neighbors, all my friends, all my relatives. Thank you for your goodness to us. Help us to always be good to each other and to all we meet. In Jesus name. Amen.

Bear one another's burdens,
and in this way you will fulfill the law of Christ.

Galatians 6:2

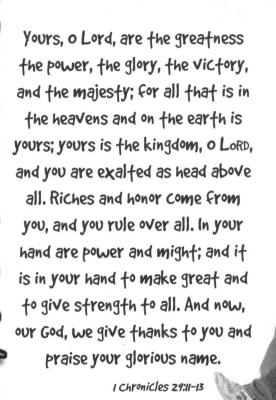

Yours, o Lord, are the greatness
the power, the glory, the victory,
and the majesty; for all that is in
the heavens and on the earth is
yours; yours is the kingdom, o LORD,
and you are exalted as head above
all. Riches and honor come from
you, and you rule over all. In your
hand are power and might; and it
is in your hand to make great and
to give strength to all. And now,
our God, we give thanks to you and
praise your glorious name.

1 Chronicles 29:11-13

MY PRAYER REQUESTS

_____

_____

_____

_____

_____

_____

_____

_____

_____

_____

_____

_____

_____

"O that I might have my request,
and that God would grant my desire."

Job 6:8

PRAYER POINT

God is faithful to hear my prayers and to answer
them in the best way possible, even if that way
is different from my requests. I can trust God
because God is trustworthy and faithful.

Awesome God, I put my trust in you.

_____

_____

_____

_____

_____

_____

_____

PRAYER PROMISE

I can do all things through him
[Christ] who strengthens me.

Philippians 4:13

You who called us to hope in your Name,
which is first of all creation,
open the eyes of our hearts
that we may know you
who alone remains Highest among the highest
and Holiest among the holy.

Save those of us who are in affliction,
have mercy on the lonely,
raise up those that are fallen,
be manifested to those that are in need,
heal the sick,
bring back those of your people that go astray.
Feed the hungry,
release our captives,
lift up those that are weak,
comfort the faint-hearted.

Clement of Rome, 1st century

I prayed today and
no answer came.
I wonder.
I wait.
I believe.
I trust.
God,
"I believe:
help Thou my
unbelief!"

Mark 9:24

57

A for **ADORATION AND PRAISE**

_____

_____

_____

_____

_____

_____

_____

This ordinary day was overflowing with happiness, surprise, and friendship. I couldn't have been any happier. . . . A day this great is an unexpected gift. Thank you, God! Amen.

> I will praise the LORD as long as I live;
>
> I will sing praises to my God all my life long.
>
> _Psalm 146:2_

C for **CONFESSION**

_____

_____

_____

_____

_____

_____

_____

Dear God,

Grades, grades, grades, I get so tired of grades! . . .
Keep my spirits up while I'm under this academic pressure, and
please let some good things come my way. Amen.

So let us not grow weary in doing what is right,

for we will reap at harvest-time, if we do not give up.

Galatians 6:9

T for THANKSGIVING

_____

_____

_____

_____

_____

_____

_____

Life-giving Lord,

Things can really happen with you in my life. I just have to smile when I think about it. Amen.

> I came that they may have life, and have it abundantly.
>
> _John 10:10b_

S for **SUPPLICATION**

_____

_____

_____

_____

_____

_____

_____

Lord, It's my turn. My report is due. I must stand in front of the class and present it. . . . Thinking about it makes me nervous, and being nervous could cause me to stumble through my presentation. I pray that I'll do well. Amen

"The Lord is my helper;
I will not be afraid.
What can anyone do to me?"
Hebrews 13:6

+ I for **INTERCESSORY**

_____

_____

_____

_____

_____

_____

_____

Eternal God, Someone I know is grieving. I'm not exactly sure what to say or do, because I don't have much experience with death. . . . I pray that you will comfort my friend and help me feel less awkward. Amen.

Bear one another's burdens,
and in this way you will fulfill the law of Christ.

Galatians 6:2

Thank you God, for not letting go. The scripture says you have a tight grip on my life, now and forever (Romans 8:38, 39). How could I not be happy and secure even on bad days? Your love accepts me as I am right here and right now, no strings attached.

I pray, O Perfect Friend, that my response to this Good News would be faith and a real freedom to love others as you have loved me. And I pray for your forgiveness and continued acceptance when I do fail to love as I should. Thank you God for the example and presence of Jesus who loved and is loving, who was so human and so divine, who will never let us go. . . . Amen.

MY PRAYER REQUESTS

_____

_____

_____

_____

_____

_____

_____

_____

_____

_____

_____

Hear, O LORD, when I cry aloud,
be gracious to me and answer me!

Psalm 27:7